Grajek z Hamelin

The Pied Piper

retold by Henriette Barkow

illustrated by Roland Dry

MANTRA LINGUA

Nie wszyscy wierzą w prawdziwość tej historii, niemniej jednak chcę ją wam opowiedzieć.

   Dawno, dawno temu istniało pewne miasteczko, zwane Hamelin. Było to zwyczajne miasteczko, które zamieszkiwali zwyczajni ludzie, tacy jak ja i ty.
   Pewnego roku miasteczko to opanowały SZCZURY. Było ich bez liku: duże i małe, tłuste i chude... Gdzie nie spojrzeć, wszędzie aż roiło się od SZCZURÓW!

Some people believe this story is true, and others that it is not. But either way this story I will tell to you.

   Many years ago, in the days of old, there was a town called Hamelin. It was an ordinary town, with ordinary people just like you and me.
   One year the town had an invasion of RATS. There were big rats and small rats, fat rats and thin rats. Wherever you looked there were RATS!

THIS BOOK BELONGS TO

....

....

....

....

FOR TINA - H.B.
FOR MY FAMILY AND FRIENDS - R.D.

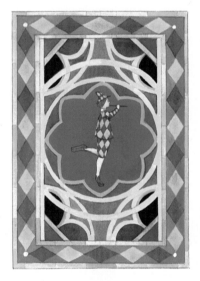

Mantra Lingua Ltd
Global House, 303 Ballards Lane, London N12 8NP
www.mantralingua.com

First Published in 2002 by Mantra Lingua Ltd
Text copyright © Henriette Barkow
Illustration copyright © 2002 Roland Dry
Dual Language Text copyright © 2002 Mantra Lingua Ltd
Audio copyright © 2009 Mantra Lingua Ltd
This sound enabled edition published 2012

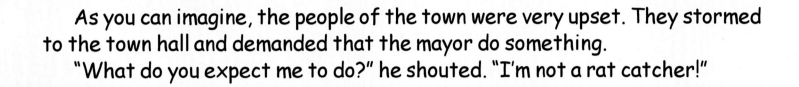

Możecie sobie wyobrazić, jak bardzo zdenerwowani byli mieszkańcy miasteczka. Popędzili do ratusza i zażądali, by burmistrz zaczął działać.

"Co mam robić?" - zawołał burmistrz. "Nie jestem szczurołapem!"

As you can imagine, the people of the town were very upset. They stormed to the town hall and demanded that the mayor do something.

"What do you expect me to do?" he shouted. "I'm not a rat catcher!"

W tej samej chwili pojawił się pewien nieznajomy przybysz, odziany w przedziwne szaty, z fletem w dłoni. Tłum zaczął wpatrywać się w niego tak, jak to często ludzie przyglądają się nieznajomym, ale jemu to wcale nie przeszkadzało.

At that very moment a stranger appeared, wearing the most unusual clothes and holding a pipe in his hand. The crowd stared at the stranger, the way that people often stare at strangers, but that didn't bother him.

Nieznajomy podszedł prosto do burmistrza i przedstawił się tymi słowy: "Nazywają mnie 'Grajkiem'. Jeśli zapłacisz mi dwadzieścia guldenów, pomogę wam pozbyć się szczurów."

Burmistrz nie posiadał się z radości. "Jeżeli naprawdę potrafisz uczynić to, co mówisz, zapłacę ci z prawdziwą radością" - odparł.

The stranger walked straight up to the mayor and introduced himself. "They call me the Pied Piper and if you pay me twenty pieces of gold I will take all your rats away."

Well this was music to the mayor's ears. "If you can truly do what you say, I shall be more than happy to pay you," he replied.

Mieszkańcy miasteczka czekali i patrzyli z uwagą. Czy ten dziwaczny grajek rzeczywiście może wypędzić wszystkie szczury? Te duże i małe? Te młode i stare?

The town's people waited and watched. Could this so called Pied Piper really get rid of all the rats - the big rats and the small rats, the young rats and the old rats?

Nieznajomy zaczął powoli grać na flecie i wówczas stało się coś niebywałego. Z każdego kącika i każdej szczeliny na ulicę zaczęły wybiegać chmary szczurów. Wszystkie one, zaklęte dźwiękami muzyki, biegły za grającym.

The Pied Piper slowly started to play his pipe and an unbelievable thing happened. From every nook and cranny the rats poured out onto the street, and under the spell of the music, they followed the piper.

Wybiegły za nim z miasta i podążyły za nim nad rzekę Weser. Nad rzeką grajek zmienił melodię: przy żałosnym zawodzeniu fletu szczury rzuciły się w lodowaty nurt i potopiły.

They followed him out of Hamelin town to the river Weser. Here, the Pied Piper changed his tune and with a mournful wailing, the rats threw themselves into the icy water and drowned.

Burmistrz Hamelin był chciwym człowiekiem i nie zamierzał zapłacić nieznajomemu ani jednego guldena. Gdy grajek przyszedł do niego po zapłatę, burmistrz roześmiał się tylko i pokręcił głową. "Skoro nie ma już szczurów, dlaczego miałbym ci płacić?!" – rzekł z przekąsem.

Now the mayor of Hamelin was a greedy man, and he wasn't going to give any money to a stranger. When the Pied Piper came and demanded his pieces of gold the mayor laughed and shook his head. "Now that the rats are gone why should I give you anything?" he snarled.

Mieszkańcy miasteczka stali wokół i przysłuchiwali się rozmowie. Nie stanęli w obronie grajka, choć wiedzieli, że burmistrz postępuje nieuczciwie. Nikt się nie odezwał.

The people stood and listened. They didn't stand up for the piper, even though they knew that their mayor was wrong. They didn't say a word.

"Zastanów się, burmistrzu!" – ostrzegł grajek. "Jeśli nie otrzymam zapłaty, sprawię, że całe miasteczko będzie cierpieć bardziej, niż można to sobie wyobrazić."

Burmistrz nie potrafił wyobrazić sobie nic gorszego od szczurów, więc odwrócił się i odszedł, wołając:
"NIE DAM CI ANI PÓŁ GULDENA!"

"Think again, mayor!" the piper warned. "If you don't pay, then I will make this town suffer more than you can ever imagine."
Well the mayor couldn't think of anything worse than the rats and so he stomped off shouting:
"I WILL NEVER PAY YOU!"

Tego samego popołudnia, podczas gdy mieszkańcy miasteczka pracowicie naprawiali szkody wyrządzone przez szczury, nieznajomy grajek stanął na placu, wolno uniósł flet do ust i zaczął grać melodię tak wdzięczną, że nie sposób opisać jej słowami.

That very afternoon, while the people were busy repairing their town, the Pied Piper stood in the town square. Slowly he lifted the pipe to his lips, and played a tune that no words could describe.

Z każdą kolejną nutką na placu pojawiało się coraz więcej dzieci, które tańczyły i śpiewały w takt muzyki.

With each new note more and more children appeared, and danced and sang to the music.

Grajek odwrócił się i wyszedł poza miasto, nie przerywając gry,
a dzieci podążyły za nim, oczarowane niezwykłą muzyką.

The Pied Piper turned and walked out of the town playing his
pipe and all the children followed, caught under the spell of
his music.

Tańcząc i śpiewając do wtóru, cały korowód podążył na wzgórze. Gdy już wydawało się, że dalej iść nie sposób, otwarły się przed nimi tajemnicze wrota.

Up the hill they danced and sang to the rhythm of the tune. When it looked like they could go no further, a door opened before them.

Dzieci, jedno po drugim, ruszyły za grajkiem i na zawsze znikły we wnętrzu wzgórza. Wszystkie oprócz jednego, które nie mogło nadążyć za innymi.

One by one the children followed the Pied Piper into the heart of the hill forever. All except one, who could not keep up with the others.

Gdy ten mały chłopiec powrócił do miasteczka, czar stracił nad nim moc. Mieszkańcy miasteczka wpatrywali się w chłopca z niedowierzaniem, gdy opowiedział im, co się wydarzyło. Zaczęli szukać i nawoływać swe dzieci, ale już nigdy więcej ich nie zobaczyli.

When the little boy returned to the town it was as if a spell had been broken. The people stared at him in disbelief when he told them what had happened. They called and cried for their children, but they never saw them again.

Key Words

town	miasteczko
people	mieszkańcy
rats	szczury
town hall	ratusz
mayor	burmistrz
rat catcher	szczurołap
stranger	nieznajomy
clothes	strój
pipe	flet
crowd	tłum
pied piper	grajek
twenty	dwadzieścia
pieces of gold	guldeny

Kluczowe słowa

music	muzyka
playing	grając
river	rzeka
greedy	chciwy
money	pieniądze
suffer	cierpieć
children	dzieci
danced	tańczyły
sang	śpiewały
rhythm	rytm
tune	melodia
hill	wzgórze
spell	czar

Legenda o tajemniczym grajku nawiązuje do wydarzeń, które miały miejsce w niemieckim miasteczku Hameln. Opowieść ta pochodzi z 1284 roku.

Więcej informacji w angielskiej wersji językowej można znaleźć na atrakcyjnej stronie internetowej miasta Hameln, pod adresem: http://www.hameln.com/englis

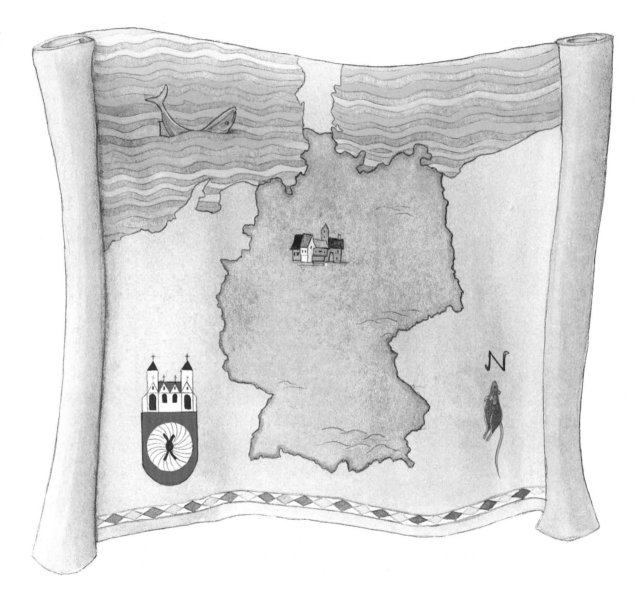

The legend of the Pied Piper originates from events that took place in the town of Hameln in Germany. The story dates back to 1284.

If you would like more information the town of Hameln has an excellent website in English: http://www.hameln.com/englis

If you've enjoyed this bilingual story in Polish & English look out for other
Mantra titles in Polish & English

Folk stories in Mantra's World Tales Series

Buskers of Bremen - adapted from the Brothers Grimm
Don't Cry Sly - adapted from Aesop's Fables
The Giant Turnip - a Russian folk story
Goldilocks and the Three Bears
Jack and the Beanstalk - an English folk story
Not Again Red Riding Hood
The Pied Piper - a German legend

Mantra's Contemporary Story Series

Alfie's Angels
Flash Bang Wheee!
Mei Ling's Hiccups
The Wibbly Wobbly Tooth

Myths and Legends in Mantra's World Heritage Series

The Children of Lir - a Celtic Myth
Pandora's Box - a Greek Myth

Mantra's Classic Story Series

What shall we do with the Boo Hoo Baby?

Many of the above books are also available on audio CD. To see the full range of Mantra's resources
do visit our website at www.mantralingua.com

QUE

THE INCREDIBLE WORM

Daniel Postgate

meadowside 🍃
CHILDREN'S BOOKS

Into a brook
Dropped a worm
on a hook.

"Bless my soul!" said a trout
with a yell.
"What a marvellous treat -
Something tasty to eat.
And I'm just getting peckish
as well!"

The worm said, "I'm tasty
But don't be too hasty,
To eat me would be a great blunder...
As a matter of fact,
I can dance, sing and act.
In a word – I'm an
            absolute wonder!"

"So the worm entertains!
 Or at least so he claims...
 Well let us be the judge," said a pike.
"We don't claim to be smart
 About theatre and art,
 But we certainly know what we like."

So the worm said, "Right-o!
Let's get on with the show!"
And he put on a tiny top hat.
And from somewhere there came
A small sparkling cane.
"It's a promising start," said a sprat.

Then the worm sang a song,
It was bold, it was strong,
And yet sentimental and sweet.
Asked a bass, "Is it wrong
To be moved by a song
From a creature I'd happily eat?"

Then straight after that
The worm started to tap.
And he tip-tapped his way
round the hook.

All the fish found his dancing
And prancing entrancing -

Soon others came
over to look.

Then the worm played guitar;
He played Blues, Rock and Ska.
He played Funk, he played Punk,
    he played Jive.
All the fish folk applauded
And felt well-rewarded
For letting the worm stay alive.

Then the worm told
those folks
Such hilarious jokes
That they howled like
they hadn't for years.

"Oh, you've tickled me pink!"
Said a freshwater shrimp
As it laughed through
its saltwater tears.

The worm smiled and bowed,
And said thanks to the crowd.
"My dear friends, you're
   a generous bunch.
Now, I really must go—"
But the trout said, "Oh no.
You're talented, clever
And funny, however...

"I still want to eat you for lunch!"

All the fish made a fuss,
They said, "What about us?"

"Don't be daft," said the trout,
   "he's too small.
Come along, let's not quibble
He's my little nibble -
I spotted him first, after all!"

Then the worm whispered sweetly,
"Before you all eat me,
Please let me perform
                    one last time...

"Gather close. **Take a look!**"
Then he climbed up the hook
And he tugged, very hard,
on the line.

With a great sudden swish
Something swung past the fish
And into a net they were bundled...

With a flip and a flop,
And a splash and a plop,
Straight into a churn
   they were tumbled!

"So now what did you think
Of the show?" asked the shrimp.
Said the trout,
"Well, I really must say...

"That young worm is a star.
Without doubt he'll go far...
At the end I was quite
swept away!"

The boy cried, "Hoorah!
That's my best catch by far!"
And he picked up his battered
old churn.
With a splosh and a splish
He went off with his fish,

And of course,
His incredible worm!

For Poppy

First published in 2012 by Meadowside Children's Books,
185 Fleet Street, London EC4A 2HS
www.meadowsidebooks.com

Text & illustrations © Daniel Postgate 2012

The right of Daniel Postgate to be identified as the author and illustrator of this work
has been asserted by him in accordance with the Copyright, Designs and Patents Act, 1988

A CIP catalogue record for this book is available from the British Library

2 4 6 8 10 9 7 5 3 1

Paper used in the production of this book is a natural,
recyclable product from wood grown in sustainable forests